How To Survive and Excel in Prison (Within and Without)

BY ABDUR-RAUF A. RASHID

Published By:

Which Way Is Out? Publications
P.O. Box 26250
Dayton, OH. 45426

Printed in the United States of America
First printing: April, 2001
Second printing: September, 2001

ISBN 0-9710607—0-3

Library of Congress Control Number:
2001091034

DEDICATION

In memory of Evelyn Dunlap, (Grandma)...
who was always there for me.

A Tribute To…

Margaret T. Nickerson, (my mother), who gave birth to my person which allows my spirit to continue. Thank you for your strength and example.

At the age of fourteen you had to drop out of the eighth grade and go to work to help "make ends meet" at home and help take care of your siblings.

As you entered into adulthood you married and had two sons. The marriage wasn't beneficial for you and your two sons, you had the strength to leave and the courage, will and love to raise your two sons alone.

At the age of thirty-two you made up your mind to over come obstacles. You started night school, (adult education), and began in the eighth grade; through time and determination you completed the twelfth grade.

You immediately, began your pursuit towards obtaining your bachelor's degree in education and succeeded in achieving it. You then excelled and obtained your Master's degree in Educational Administration. After thirty-four years in the classroom at the age of seventy-four, you are still teaching and positively influencing the many children who pass through your fourth grade classroom. You continue to do that which you love to do so much. Thank you for touching so many lives, and above all, thank you for touching mine.

Thank you Edward G. Dunlap,(my big brother), whose guidance and love gave me strength and a "will" to succeed!

A very special acknowledgment to my loving wife, Latonya Rashid, whose support, encouragement and computer skills helped bring this work together. Additionally, to my loving children Sefu, Sidney, and Casey who were patient while their dad was transposing his thoughts onto paper.

I sympathize/empathize with all of humanity locked behind

America's prison doors. Also, the families and loved ones yearning for their freedom.

A very special thanks and appreciation to Shekhem-T Seshmi-T Maat aka Jamillah Talibah for her sincere interest and dedication in editing this work and helping bring it to its completion.

A very special thanks to Stacey Wilder for her technical support and typesetting skills.

A deep appreciation and admiration for Ra un Nefer Amen I whose direction showed me the "opening of the way".

Thank you Charlene Selmer-Jones for your support and enthusiasm in seeing this project to completion.

I wish to express special gratitude to our very talented web site designer, Mr. David C. Ward. Thank you Mr. Anthony and Mrs. Evelyn Ward for your earnest support in this project.

Thank you and deep appreciation to Sam and Connie Melson for your encouragement.

Lastly, but surely not least, I acknowledge my Creator. I'm thankful for life, light and determination.

About the Author... After years of being incarcerated and regaining my freedom, I never have nor ever will forget that experience. I've always found the need to volunteer and go back into the penitentiaries of America and hope to try to make a difference for all the human beings that are still locked behind the prison walls.

In embracing that enormous task, I have felt compelled to put these few thoughts down in writing and share some of my past experiences of incarceration with who ever is willing to read them, "How To Survive And Excel In Prison". Not only are these thoughts intended for the incarcerated human beings of America and elsewhere, but also for those family members, loved ones and friends on the outside who are concerned about those who are confined behind prison walls and barbed wire fences.

The words and thoughts contained in this discussion will, hopefully, shed some light and understanding on what prison life is and can be, both positive and negative, constructive or destructive.

We will discuss some of the truths of prison life and hopefully, dispel the myth of... "once a criminal, always a criminal". I began my life behind prison walls when I was 19 years of age and concluded my prison experience when I was 32 years of age. I spent all but 9 months of my twenties behind prison walls. I was granted parole in 1974 from a twenty year sentence for armed bank robbery, after serving four years, 6 months, when I was paroled from Petersburg Federal Reformatory. In July of 1975, I was charged and sentenced to a brand new twenty year sentence for armed bank robbery where I was tried as an adult and sentenced to twenty years in Atlanta Federal Penitentiary while still on parole.

During this second twenty year sentence, while in Atlanta Federal penitentiary I had another person, who was also incarcerated, (a jailhouse lawyer) read and study my court transcripts. He found a flaw in the allegations of bank robbery, *aiding and abetting*, which I was also given a twenty year sentence for that ran concurrent with the sentence for armed bank robbery. Yet, I was the *only* one charged for the crime.

The "jailhouse lawyer" appealed my case for me to the United States Supreme Court. I won that appeal! My length of time did not change, although the twenty year sentence for aiding and abetting was vacated.

My case made precedent and can, to this day, be found in The Federal Reporter 577, page 867; United Sates of America Vs. Lenear Charles Dunlap.

I am considered what's known as " a two time loser" and for all practical purposes I should have been chalked up by all sociological and criminal statistics, as being destined to a total life of crime and recidivism. However, I chose to dispel that concept and consider myself, "a two time winner".

I hope that as you journey through these chapters, you will come to understand my meaning!

During the years of my imprisonment I have served time in many of America's penal institutions, such as, Baltimore City Jail, Mecklinburg County Jail, El Reno OK. Federal Reformatory, Terre Haute Federal Penitentiary, Petersburg Federal Reformatory, Atlanta Federal Penitentiary, Danbury Federal Corrections Inst., Levenworth KS. Federal Penitentiary, Oxford WI. Federal Corrections Inst., Lewisburg Federal Penitentiary and Lexington Ky. Federal Corrections Inst.

I was blessed to come through it all, safely, with my intelligence manhood intact. I obtained several college degrees while in prison the second time. I received degrees in the field of culinary arts; Hotel and Restaurant Management, Hotel and Restaurant Cookery with a minor in psychology.

My very first job, upon being paroled and reentering into

society, was an assistant manager's position at a major fast food restaurant where my beginning salary was $18,000.00 yearly. There are many companies and corporations that have special programs set up to assist in viable job placements for Viet Nam vets and ex-felons. This was one such program.

I am now employed with a major airline. I work in marketing and sales where I have been employed for over 16 years. I am also actively engaged in the pursuit of a degree in Urban Affairs, Criminal Justice. I aspire to be a Warden in one of America's penitentiaries where I hope to make a positive contribution to all concerned.

May my life, words, and "being" have meaning and grant light...!

How to contact the author:

Mr. Abdur-Rauf A. Rashid
Which Way Is Out? Publications
P.O. Box 26250
Dayton, OH 45426

Web site: http://www.wwiopublications.com

Table of Contents

On Courtside

This particular phase of your new judicial experience can be full of positive anticipation for you or be filled with a feeling of doom; that life has come to an end. Of course, any person in his/her right mind hopes to walk out of the court room a free man or woman when the trial is over and the verdict is read: "not guilty"!

As mentioned before, you can be filled with anticipation of a positive outcome simply because you know (fully and without a doubt) that you are totally innocent of the crime you've been charged. So, if justice prevails, you should most likely be found "not guilty" and freed of all charges... however, I'm sure you know that this idealistic concept isn't always 100% fool proof.

Conversely, you could be filled with unrealistic optimism anticipating a favorable outcome, knowing full well that you are guilty as charged and the evidence is stacked against you.

Inspite of your guilt, you hope for a judicial technicality or some miracle to occur that would allow you to walk out of the court room a free man or free woman.

Now, please don't misunderstand the point that I am attempting to convey here. Of course you want to regain your freedom, certainly don't want to be incarcerated, by all means, hope for that judicial technicality that will allow you to experience that miracle of freedom. However, by the same token...***TO THINE OWN SELF BE TRUE!***

While you are on courtside it would be very important for you to examine how you conduct yourself. Give it some thought... what are your habits, adhering to the institutions rules, are you staying free of contraband, are you focused on preparing yourself to do "time" in a constructive manner.

You see the mind-state and habits that were with you during your court side time will be the "baggage" that you will take into the penitentiary to really do your "time".

Who Are You? A Criminal?

(Beware of the Label)

So, who are you? Really think about this question for a moment. So, here you are, your trial is over. No judicial technicalities and miracles of freedom... you've been found guilty and sentenced to serve "time". That makes you a criminal or does it?

The word Criminal - as defined by Webster's Collegiate Dictionary (tenth addition) is 1: guilty of crime.2: a person who has been convicted of a crime. 3: Disgraceful.

Labels are either self-imposed or given by someone else, be it by another individual, group of individuals or by society it self. Some labels can be considered stigmas, i.e., thief, murderer, rapist, convict and etc.

Labels can be character building or on the contrary be, a destroyer of character. Who are you? you may go by the name of John, Ralph, Mary, Muhammad, Elizabeth, Heru or Jamillah, etc. and you identify with that name.

You must realize that you are comprised of many labels, you are father, mother, son, daughter, husband, wife, worker, provider and on and on. All of these labels have certain innate characteristics or qualities and certain connotations of what the name or label implies, but they are just labels. You are a human being, man, woman you have a gender.

Now comes along some more labels such as criminal, convict, murderer, rapist, thief, baller, etc. Which of course are in stark contrast to the more positive labels that were earlier mentioned i.e., mother, father ,worker and so on. Yet, none of these labels are really "you". "***You***, being your "***true essence***".

What is your "***true essence***"? You possess the spirit of the Creator. Your "***true essence***" separates you from the animal kingdom. It's that which allows you to exercise your "will", to do that which is right or that which is wrong.

You were born just like every other human being on the face of this planet. And that was through the agency of your mother's womb. Every president, preacher, priest, imam (Muslim Minister), doctor, lawyer or judge was brought forth through creation this way. So, are you starting to get my point?

You were born in the likeness of all that is good, that which possesses greatness, with unlimited potential. That which is more essential than a mere label or name. That's who you are! You are that which is able to "become"—but, become what? In the following chapters we will have a clear and concise answer to that question.

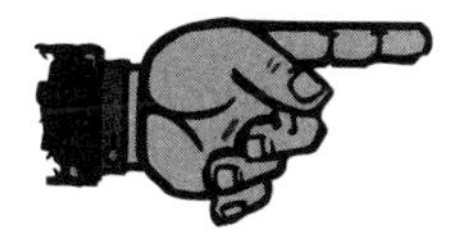

Who's to Blame For My Being Here?

You know, pointing a finger and casting blame is one of man's most convenient tools. It relieves us of responsibility, accountability and, unfortunately, sometimes from reality. I'm sure that all of us who have been or who are incarcerated have had or have a sad song to sing and "a violin to play" regarding the reason for our incarceration. I know for a fact that I had mine. As mentioned in the opening of this discussion, I didn't hesitate to tell you that I had been incarcerated in the state and federal penitentiaries of America.

As a young man in my early 20's in the penitentiary I did a lot of pointing of the finger as to the reason why I was in jail. I blamed my criminal activity and drug use on the fact that I came from a broken home, had no fatherly figure for guidance, etc., etc., etc.

etc., etc.

After some years passed whereby I continued blaming others, not accepting the unproductive choices that I made which lent to my incarceration (imprisonment), I gained some enlightenment. I gained this new awareness by really looking at my life, my past environment and upbringing. I gave a long hard and unbiased look! Let me explain—I only have one brother who is older than me by four years.

My parents divorced when I was twelve, which would have made my brother sixteen years of age at the time. So, by my being the youngest, you can imagine how much trouble my older brother must have gotten himself into and how much time he must have served, because after all we lived in a rough environment, had no father image, and drugs were easy to find.

Guess what? None of the above applies to my brother! My older brother grew up in the same environment that I did and experienced the same, if not more, pressures than I did. After all, he was, for all practical purposes, the "man" of the house. He had to help my mother with the bills. God bless my mother, who did the best she possibly could, but that is a whole different topic of discussion in itself.

My brother had the challenge of getting money to help my mother, who was going to night school at the age of 32, having dropped out of school in the 8th grade. She was trying to do better for us. How did my older brother get money? He worked for it. He had a job. He was determined not to be suckered into the tricks and traps of society and end up in the jailhouses of America.

I could go on and on about my mother and brother whom I love very dearly, but to make a long story shorter, my brother, retired from the Baltimore City Police Department after 32 years of Service, as Sergeant Detective in 1999.

Why didn't my brother resort to a life of crime? Why didn't he go to jail? Why did I? It's not very hard to really understand...simply...we made choices. We, as human beings, are able to make choices with the free will that the "Creator", (or whatever name you choose to use, that's comfortable for you) has allowed us as human beings to possess.

I chose to smoke reefer, I chose to snort heroine and coke. I chose to shoot those drugs into my veins. I also, chose to jump those bank counters and get money. I too, unconsciously, chose to go to jail.

When I really began to think about it, how did I figure that I could continue to break the laws of man and, above all the laws of "The Creator", by acting other than as my "true self", and not pay the heavy consequences of imprisonment, destitution or even death? You see, right is right and wrong is wrong...and that's "cut and dry".

So, remember, just watch yourself when you point your finger to try to place blame. When you're pointing one finger out, three are pointing back at you! Find the true answers as to who is really the blame for your being incarcerated.

Starting Your Sentence (The First Day)

R & D stands for receiving and discharge. This place can be the most undesirable place you could ever want to be or it can be the place where you could be happiest. I say that it's the most undesirable place for the mere fact that the reality is setting in that you're in the penitentiary and about to be introduced into the general population of individuals who have been in there from one day to 40, 50 years and more.

Now, I don't care how "bad" we think we are or how good we can handle ourselves or who we already know that's in there, you are still going to be uncomfortable, insecure and down right scared! Be real! You know you are scared, but it's OK you're human.

So, now the systematic stripping away of your identity begins by the institution itself. The first thing you do is sit in a holding cell or area for an hour or two waiting to be finger printed and processed in, and don't let the shift be changing for count time, you just might sit there three hours! You are then greeted by the "hack" (C.O.), correction's officer in charge of R & D and told to strip butt naked, then the C.O. takes one of many memorable trips up the crack of your behind, aided by your hands which are willing to hold it open as the search for contraband continues. Who knows you might have a 357 magnum up there or something! Then you're told to open your mouth wide and poke out and lift your tongue and the C.O. goes behind your ears, under your armpits, up under your genitals and even to the bottom of your feet. Somewhat humiliating, huh? We're not finished yet. Now its time to take a shower with "state soap", In many cases you are then fumigated for lice and other parasites that you may or may not be carrying around with you.

Then you're given your prison garb (clothes), some bare essentials such as a toothbrush, toothpaste, blanket, towel and wash cloth and last but not least, a booklet of do's and don'ts that welcomes you to your new society. Needless to say, this is the place where you will be residing for the x number of months, years, or decades to come. Oh! Don't forget the most important thing that the institution can give you is your *new* number! You are subliminally stripped of your identity and given a new label known as a number. Those who may have served in the military are probably familiar with this process. However, that is not the focus of this discussion.

Who's Your Friend?

You must remember that when you first walk into that prison population, you have no friends! You need to deal with all of your fellow inmates with "long-handled spoons". Remember, a smile is just a frown turned upside down. Prison life, for some is merely survival. You are in a society of men/women, or in some weird prison settings co-ed, such as, in the Lexington, KY. Federal Prison.

Regardless of the prison environment, one will find that it's the most unnatural existence on the face of the earth. The co-ed facility wasn't that much different because the rules there stated that the most the male and female inmates could do was talk or hold hands...Yeah...right!!! Because we all know, where there's a will, there's a way. Remember, friendships developed in prison are not automatic.

First Impressions

Your first impression when you go out into population is very important. Above all, do not be naive. Don't accept anything from another inmate, especially if you don't know them. Check out your environment, mentally, because it's going to take awhile before you find out who means you good or bad. The less you talk and converse with other inmates for the first few weeks or so, the better. People won't be able to read you or pick up weaknesses or vulnerabilities. Silence is "golden".

Your Caseworker...
Your Best Friend or Worst Enemy!

Once you are in general population and begin your orientation you will soon meet your caseworker. Your case worker is responsible for logging your progress while you're confined and also will help you set up a structure of activity; be it work, school, programming, or enrolling in the various programs offered, etc.

By all means establish a respectful relationship with your caseworker. Remember, your case worker is a human being and has a job to do. No one wants his/her job made difficult! So, if at all possible make your caseworker your friend or at least a respected associate. Regardless of how much time you have, the caseworker will be the person who will be influencing the parole board either positively or negatively as far as your chances of getting "out" are concerned.

Choices

This is a simple topic, not difficult to understand. Obviously you know what choices you made to get your freedom taken away from you, so hence forth you need to rely on your better judgment to help you work your way out of the mess your previous choices got you into.

State of Asceticism

Asceticism as defined by Webster's Collegiate Dictionary (tenth addition), 1; practicing strict self-denial as a measure of personal discipline esp. spiritual discipline.

Usually, when you hear the term asceticism, one thinks of deep and selfless devotion, the thoughts are focused on the higher self and of the metaphysical workings of the universe... yeah, I know... "deep" huh! But, not really.

When you look at the great individuals in the history of man you can see this ascetic behavior. For example, the great prophets and teachers of the world such as Sidhartha Gautama, left all the world he knew, gave it up, went deep into the woods and lived there for a vast amount of time alone. He fasted and prayed for long periods of time, and thus became the Buddha, (the Enlightened One).

How about Moses, who went up on Mount Sinai, for long periods of time to be alone and returned as, The Leader of Men.

Let's take a look at Jesus, who left his surroundings for eighteen years from the time he was 12 years of age until the age of thirty who then went out into the wilderness for vast periods of time until he became the Christ, "Light of the Worlds".

Then we have Muhammad, who gave up all of his wealth and went to the cave of Hira and spent vast amounts of time praying and fasting until he became the "Seal of Prophethood".

All of these individuals had something in common, they wanted to make a change and a change for the good. They wanted to learn the real aspects of life and death.

This greatness that these individuals possessed all came about after shedding the shackles of the world around them and really attempting to "see". They achieved "light", became "enlightened" and went on to change the world.

Of course there are many other great men and women past and present. One comes to mind whom many of us are aware of, and that is none other than Malcolm X, as many of us know him. Was he in prison? Did he study, educate himself, exercise discipline and excel in prison? When he was released, did he have great impact in the world? Yes!

So, here you are in prison, locked away from the hustle and bustle of the outside world. Yes, there are still others around you in that environment. However, when the lights go out at night and everything is quiet except, for a few occasional snores emanating from around you from the cell block or dorm. When it's dark and quiet, there is no one there, but you and God, (The Creator).

This is the time when quite a few tears are shed, when out of sight of fellow inmates and guards, but in the sight of God and our own hearts! That quiet time, late at night, should serve as your time to reinforce your discipline and be prepared for the next day of life in the penitentiary. You must seize this time to search for your own answers. But, if you don't have questions...you can't hope to find answers. Due to the mere fact that you are physically locked-up, makes it certain that you have questions...seek the answers from within.

How Do I Do This Time?

You do it wisely! One day at a time you have to get into a mind-set. You have to get a focus and a purpose. Your focus can be positive (constructive) or negative (destructive). I strongly suggest that it should be positive.

What Human Resources Are Available?

Making the decision to take the positive approach to doing your time, you have to check out the human resources available to you. What are human resources? A resource is something that is available to care for a need. In this regard, a human need. An example of a natural resource would be oil, natural gas, etc.

What human resources are available to you in the institution where you are confined? The educational resources at your disposal, range from G.E.D. prep to college, graduate work, or computer science.

Various religious resources are available to you, such as Judaism, Christianity, Islam, Ausarian/Khamitian, etc. You might find such programs as A.A./N.A., 7 Steps, Jaycee's, etc.

What employment opportunities are available to you, which might allow you to earn a wage? Believe me, there are not many prisons which don't offer some type of industry or means of manufacture because, whether you realize it or not, you are a commodity. Prisons can be and are big business, be they state or federal. You are cheap labor; at least use it to your advantage. You might as well.

Also, check out the food service job opportunities, laundry, infirmary, janitorial, the educational department, etc. There are plenty of job opportunities, which will allow you to earn wages in your prison environment.

Another, equally important, resource is recreational. What recreational resources are at your disposal? You simply have to look into the word to see the value in it. Yes, to *recreate* yourself by doing something that you enjoy, that is positive such as, running, exercising, weight training, meditating, playing cards (not gambling), shooting pool, reading, hobbies, etc.

An important tool to use in "doing your time", is goal setting. Yes, set goals for yourself. If you don't have a G.E.D., then set a goal to get it! Then set a goal to begin college courses, set goals to start and complete various trades. Set goals not to get caught up in the tricks and traps of prison life, which are so prevalent in the day-to-day life in that environment.

We'll be discussing some of those undesirables in up coming chapters. Above all, set positive goals. Even if you have life and a day, still set your goals for positive accomplishments, and never, ever give up hope. You must stay focused. Spend time in the law library studying and educating yourself. Read, become disciplined in striving for positivity—it's your environment and it's up to you to make it livable or unlivable.

The Appeal Process

According to due process, every person convicted of a crime is allowed the appeal process. Just because you are sentenced does not, necessarily mean that you're going to keep the jail sentence that you were given. Remember the miracle of freedom that we discussed earlier, well miracles do happen. Guilty verdicts can be over turned and new trials can be granted if the criteria for such an event are met. By all means, exhaust all remedies concerning your appeal process, it's a constitutional right.

Scenario: Here you are serving your time, you've been "down" seven months. One morning a C.O. in the chow line at breakfast pulls you out of the line and accuses you of going through the line twice. You know that you are being dealt with unjustly, because this is your first time going through the line, but the C.O. won't hear it, he or she still tells you to get out of line. So, you mouth off at the C.O., he grabs you, a scuffle ensues then the "goon squad" is called and you get locked-down in the hole.

So, what came of this encounter? Well, you surely got your point across to the guard. Also, now you possibly have brand new charges: assault on a C.O., inciting a riot, etc. Even though you may have been in the right, what do you think is going to happen to your appeal? How is your "jacket" going to look even if you do win your appeal and get a new trial...with a *new* penitentiary charge?

Do you think that the incident with you and the C.O. is not going to follow you on your record? You have to think and be disciplined under all circumstances, to get through the "time".

Communication With The Outside

Communication with the outside world, whether through written correspondence or phone, is very important. It can boost the morale and in some instances help one maintain his or her sanity behind prison walls.

We all have family and loved ones who we left or were taken away from due to our incarceration. Getting a letter is important, and the phone call is the next best thing to a visit. But, there is an important factor that you have to realize, and that is...*the whole world does not revolve around you.*

Hey Man! Get Off The Phone It's My Turn

During the years that I was imprisoned, I saw pretty bad things happen because of that phone. If policy is properly applied in the institution where you are or will be, every one who wants their routine phone call should be able to have it.

Phone calls are a privilege and can be taken away due to disciplinary problems. Speaking of discipline—you must be disciplined in the use of the phone.

For instance, let's say you call once a week or more to the outside, whether it's your mother, wife, husband, or other family members, it's a good feeling when the operator puts you through, thanks to the fact that your call is being accepted on the other end. So, you talk and talk, as the months and years go by, and eventually the calls are not accepted.

Now, it's not necessarily that you are no longer loved or cared about, it's just that folks can't afford that damn high phone bill. Phone bills of $200.00 to $300.00 or more a month that you are causing with those calls.

Remember, our families and loved ones still have to live day by day on the outside and that extra bill (burden) that you are causing with that extra high phone bill does not help.

The Dear John

This is the most dreaded correspondence that one can receive, (next to hearing of the death of a loved one or your appeal has been denied), while in the penitentiary.

You know she has tried to stick with you as long as she could, but you must realize that absence, plus time plus Jody (got your girl and gone), catches up to the relationship between you and your lady or man. At mail call you receive your "Dear John" letter.

So, now that you've got it, what are you going to do with all that hurt and anger? Go Off!!! Nope, that won't help you at all other than putting you deeper into the penitentiary.

So, do you write her back a threatening letter? Nope; that can get you another charge, and obviously she was not afraid to write you the "Dear John" in the first place.

Check this out! When I got my "Dear John", it hit me in the "gut" like a ton of bricks! I was crushed! And yes, it hurts, you feel helpless. I simply took a deep breath, slowed my breathing down and allowed myself to calm down. When the doors hit after count to go to the chow hall, I went straight to the yard and I ran 10 miles straight without stopping until I ran my frustration off. In effect, I *recreated* myself...remember—*recreation.*

To make a long story short, the woman who wrote me the "Dear John" eventually married someone else and named her first son after me, and to this day we still have kept in contact over twenty-five years later. We're still friends. So, please understand that there is still hope, and life, even after the "Dear John".

The Importance of Written Communication

Written communication is important for several reasons. Firstly, it is important to stay connected with your loved ones on the outside. If by chance you don't have family or a loved one to write to, then it might be good for you to get a "pen pal".

There are several ways to come up with a "pen pal", such as, going through a particular religious organization or affiliation, through newspapers or magazines, etc.

Secondly, written communication is important because it allows you to put your thoughts down on paper, express yourself and even purge feelings. You can release stress by writing.

Thirdly, written communication is important simply because it's just down right more economical! Compare a 34 cent stamp, 10 cents worth of writing paper, and a 6 cent envelope to a phone bill of 200.00 to 300.00 dollars a month. In other words, give your people "a break". In the following chapter we'll discuss in further detail the repercussions of these high phone bills.

The Commissary

The commissary is the penitentiary's own, in-house store or super market. For all practical purposes, it's the "only store in town"!

At the commissary you can purchase anything from jogging suits, tennis shoes, toiletries, magazines, refreshments, snacks, ice cream, etc., etc., etc. As with most stores the commissary is there to make a profit. Like most stores on the outside, prices are high. Don't think that the prison commissary is any different with their prices. They can set their own prices. But, to be fair and objective, in the various penitentiaries that I have been in across America the commissary prices are pretty much in line with prices on the outside.

Do you remember the discussion on the importance of written communication, and the high phone bills in the last chapter? Now, ponder this: Suppose you wrote more, called less and didn't run up $200.00 or $300.00 a month phone bills! By chance, do you suppose that someone would be able to send you more money to post to your commissary account?

You can't necessarily "have your cake and eat it too"! Do you expect to talk on the phone 200.00 to 300.00 dollars a month and then expect that same person to send you money to post to your commissary account?

Once again, remember, *the whole world does not revolve around you!* Furthermore, as mentioned in a previous earlier chapter, you can seek constructive employment in the different departments within the prison, earn wages, and put your own money on the books for commissary.

Beware Of The Two For One Stores

The Two For One Stores are really hustles that are set up by other inmates on your particular unit, dorm, or cell block. The Two For One Store is really self-explanatory, whatever you get from that store you owe back double.

For instance, if you borrow a pack of cigarettes on Monday you owe 2 packs when it's time for you to go to the commissary. If you don't "pay up" on the agreed upon day, the two packs double to 4 packs and so on. This is true for anything that you borrow from the Two For One Store.

My advice is to stay clear of those stores if at all possible, furthermore, those types of stores are *illegal.*

The Three Cardinal Sins

First, stay away from *drugs* (contraband). Needless to say, drugs do exist in the prison environment. You must realize that in the penal setting, you are in a society, composed of either men or in the case of a woman's prison, a society of women. To explain life in a penitentiary it can be said: where "there's a will, there's a way," to get drugs or anything else inside for that matter.

There are those incarcerated who have life-plus sentences and, of course, there are those with less time. This is a very unnatural society, a society composed of one gender, either male or female, no children, no babies, no opposite sex, etc.

Once again it would be to your benefit to stay free and clear of the drugs and such contraband.

Secondly, *homosexuality* - This is a real touchy subject both in the penitentiary as well as in the free world. Of course, being deprived of life's basic wants, (I did not say needs), needs are necessities such as food, clothing and shelter.

The human sexual drive is not too far off, but we can live

without it, even though it's "hard".

It's "hard", yeah, so what else is new. This is what generally happens when you're in an unnatural environment where you are away from a woman, or the opposite sex. Once in this unnatural setting such as prison one can somewhat lose grips with reality when it comes to basic wants, such as gratifying sexual desires. I am of the opinion that there is no excuse for imagining a grown man as a woman. Not unless you are homosexual or bisexual.

Of course, you will have those who are, by life style, either homosexual or bisexual housed within the prisons who chose this life style on the outside.

In the years that I have spent in the penal institutions of America, I've seen men who on the outside would not possibly think of a homosexual act, but when put within a prison situation, they have little or no control, discipline or inhibitions.

Just because your "joint" gets "hard", does not mean that this is a green light for you to go "butt" hunting. Often times the hunter can end up being captured by the game. I'm sure you understand what is implied here.

For those who feel they can't help but indulge in the homosexual activities that go on behind prison walls, let me give you a dose of staunch reality...whether you are the "stickee" or the "sticker" or the "giver or the "receiver", you are still both *homosexuals.* The definition of homosexuality as defined by the Webster's Collegiate dictionary (tenth addition) 1:Of, relating to, or characterized by a tendency to direct sexual desire toward another of the same sex. 2: Of, relating to, or involving sexual intercourse between persons of the same sex.

For those who are of the opinion that unless you've been in the prison situation, then one cannot speak on this topic, I somewhat agree with that opinion. However, and be mindful *that I can speak* on this subject. I was given two completely different twenty year sentences during different times in my life and served time on both of them. In fact, I've served over twelve years on the inside. Out of all the years of my confinement, never, ever did I indulge in any homosexual activity of any type, at all. The way I view it is, if a person is homosexual in the first place upon entering the prison environment then that's bad enough, because they have got their work cut out for them. But, if you're so-called straight/heterosexual, why are you going to allow the prison situation to strip you of your manhood by indulging in homosexuality?

What is one man thinking when he is having intercourse with another man? One has to use some awful vivid imagining to mistake a grown man for a woman. When one is engrossed in that homosexual act and is aroused to that state called ecstasy, what is stopping the partner from reversing the situation and performing the same act on that partner? Don't put yourself in those situations.

Yeah man, I know it's "hard", but there are other means of releasing that sexual energy. The "Creator" allowed a man a natural release mechanism commonly known as a "wet dream".

When you experience a "wet dream" it's the next best thing to being there! However, if you can't wait for the "wet dream" to roll around, then you have the ability to "take things into your own hands". I don't advocate masturbation, however, masturbation, is still the lesser of the two evils. Furthermore, sodomy, in prison is a crime, it's illegal!

At this point I find it important to dispel the myth that every man participates in homosexual activities *while in prison.* That is a lie! In fact, homosexual activity is the exception rather than the rule.

Third, and lastly, stay away from *green money* (contraband). In the prison environment green is quite simply just that... $1.00, $5.00,$10.00,$20.00 and $100.00 bills. I never will forget my first day in the penitentiary in Georgia. I was placed in an eight man "tank", which is a large cell with 8 bunks in it. I sat and watched an inmate count out $1,500.00 in cash and a half pound of reefa'(marijuana).

Just as drugs can find their way into the prison environment, so too can green money. Green money induces the need for or desire for gambling, in order to win more money.

As we all know, in gambling there has to be a winner and a loser. Green money has a higher purchasing power than does packs or cartons of cigarettes for the purchase of various contraband that is for sale in the prison environment.

Once again, green money is contraband in most prisons, which makes it illegal.

Why do I call *drugs, homosexuality*, and *green money* the "three cardinal sins"? First, as mentioned before, they are illegal and indulging them can increase your prison sentence.

Secondly, utilizing any of the three can be damaging to your well being. Thirdly, and I can say without a doubt, that most, if not all, of the murders, maiming, and strife between human-beings confined behind prison walls has to do with drugs, a homosexual, or green money...think about it!

The Infamous "Hole"

The term "hole" is another slang term for prison segregation or solitary confinement. A person is placed in the "hole" when he or she blatantly violates a rule in that particular prison environment. You usually have to commit a major infraction to be sent to the "hole". I can't think of very many reasons why a person should have to go to the "hole", other than defending themselves from harm; not being the instigator to cause the conflict.

You see...in my opinion, going to the "hole" is one of the most stupid, ignorant and undisciplined measures that a human being could allow to happen to them while already locked behind prison bars. Why? Let's examine it!

OK, you've been sentenced to serve time in prison and had your freedom taken away. You're locked up—so now that you are locked up behind prison walls you're going to get yourself *re-locked* up, even more so, (within the prison itself) in solitary confinement! Now, that's stupid!

Obviously, you haven't grasped the concept or either you have absolutely no plans to ever go in front of the parole board. If I am viewing the actions of going to the "hole" in this way, how do you think your caseworker and prison staff are viewing your actions. Think about it!

I must admit that I was sent to the "hole" once out of all the years I served in prison. This is what happened—I was in Atlanta Federal Penitentiary and it was my day to go to the commissary. I was aware that I had at least $300.00 "on the books" of my commissary account.

I was out of everything, no toothpaste, soap, deodorant, etc. As I went through the commissary line and got up to the cashier, I had about $150.00 worth of goods. I was about to get my commissary totaled and bagged so I could get my stuff back to my cell, when the commissary clerk (staff) pulled my card and told me that I didn't have any money. I asked him to check again because I knew I had at least $300.00 "on the books". He called me a liar and told me to get out of the line, and told the commissary helper to start putting my stuff back on the shelves. I told him that, "I wasn't moving and he'd better check my account and give me my commissary".

So, the two of us had a few choice words! He happened to be behind a Plexiglas partition, which allowed the inmates to see the items that they wanted to buy. At the end of the line, your items were bagged and the guard gave you your commissary.

As I think back, I'm glad that he was behind that glass partition and I couldn't get to him, because I was banging on the glass! Yes. I went off!!! I knew I was right, but being right is no excuse to be "played out of pocket". To make another long story shorter, he called the "goon squad", who came in full riot gear and escorted me to the "hole". When a person is sent to the "hole", one can expect to stay a minimum of 10 days or up to months and years, depending on the offense.

What I did in that commissary line was pretty serious from the stand point that I tried to get through the glass to get to the commissary clerk, who was prison staff. There were at least 50 to 60 other men (inmates) in line with me wanting to get their commissary who were becoming aggravated with the clerk. As well, I could have been charged with "inciting a riot". So, how long did I stay in the "hole"? I stayed in the "hole" exactly one hour. Which I was more than surprised about, because I thought for sure that I'd be looking at least 30 days in solitary confinement.

Once in the "hole", I asked my segregation officer to call my caseworker. He did.

When my caseworker came to see me in the "hole", he asked me what happened—and I told him. He then told me that he wanted to check things out and left. About 20 minutes later, he came back and told the guard in charge of solitary confinement to let me out. So, I stayed a total of one hour in the "hole".

Remember, it was established in an earlier chapter, that your caseworker can be your best friend or worst enemy. So, how does your caseworker become your best friend? (I'm using this concept of "best friend" loosely, I'm sure you grasp my point). Neither by kissing your caseworker's ass, nor by brown-nosing, or being a flunky, nor by snitching.

You do it by simply being a man and adhering to prison policy. By giving respect and expecting respect. It's as simple as that. My caseworker's very words were: "This is not like you Dunlap, (my former name), this is out of character for you. I've never had a disciplinary problem out of you. I did check the front accounting office and it's true, you do have $300.00 "on the books" that was late getting posted; but that doesn't excuse your actions, so don't let this happen again!" I agreed that I allowed myself to get put into that situation and that I appreciated his input.

Now, if I were, what's known as a "prison screw up", and frequently sent to the "hole", I would have spent a much longer time in solitary confinement.

Please, don't misunderstand the point that I am trying to make here, it's true that many incarcerated individuals would say that the "hole" is just another part of the penitentiary, and that's true. It's not that you are afraid to go to the "hole", but going to the "hole" does not enhance your chances of regaining your freedom any quicker.

In fact, it will help keep you away from your children and loved ones even longer, because all of the negatives go right into your "jacket" that the parole board will review. That's what you should be afraid of! So, stay out of the "hole"!

The Visit

The visit, can be one of your most important privileges. During a visit you have a brief time to escape from your day-to-day prison reality and be with your loved one's for however long your visit will last.

You may have noted that I said that your visit can be one of your most important privileges. Privileges can be taken away. Do you know that your visits can be denied if you're in the "hole"? Do you know that your visit can be denied if your visitor attempts to introduce contraband of any type i.e., drugs, money, weapons, etc. into the institution? Not only will your visit be denied, but your visitor could soon meet the same fate that you are experiencing. That of incarceration!

A visit can be therapeutic, if you allow it to be. When you are with your family and loved ones, make your discussions positive; such as how the children are doing in school, or how the other family members are doing, etc. Keep it on a positive note.

A visit can be disruptive when (and I've seen it happen all too many times and have been guilty of it myself), while in the visiting room, we hold our wives/woman's hands and look them in their eyes and ask them if they are seeing anybody else, or if they are cheating on us! Don't we do that!

Whether she has or she hasn't—if she tells you "yes", is that going to make it easier to do your time? Don't sit there and drill her on things because: "there *ain't* a whole lot you can do about it"! Now is there? You really should be grateful and appreciative that you got a visit, because when the visit is over, you go back to general population and she walks out the front door. At that point you should contemplate, "God, grant me the serenity to accept the things I cannot change, courage to change the things I can, and the wisdom to know the difference"!

Don't try to have your family, loved ones, or friends bring you contraband during a visit. If you were to request this of them, then you would be the "lowest of the low". I say this because, for you to do that would make it obvious that you didn't care about the repercussions of your actions for yourself; moreover it would be evident that you don't really care about your loved ones or friends either. They would be subject to prosecution for introducing contraband into the prison environment, so now you've got somebody else locked-up! This happens because in your little mind-set, the "*whole world revolves around you*"! And it's "*all about you and what you want*". Don't put your loved ones and friends in that situation!

Will I *Ever* Get Out?

Well, that really depends on you! As aforementioned, I had two completely separate twenty year sentences; one twenty year sentence as a youth and the other as an adult. I was paroled off of my first twenty year sentence, stayed "out" for nine months and caught a brand new 20 year sentence for armed bank robbery, again.

Even though this was a pretty substantial amount of time to serve, nevertheless, I maintained my faith and optimism regarding an eventual re-entry into society. I knew that I could still see "light at the end of the tunnel". I knew I had some time to do, but I felt that eventually, if I stayed focused on the positive, that I, eventually would see the "light of day"—freedom!

But, how about those who have 50 years, 80 years or multiple life sentences or who are even on death row? I can truly say that I do "feel you", and no I haven't been confronted with the true possibility of never getting out of prison, even though *anyone* housed within the prison populations of America lives with that threat on a daily basis.

Whether you have 3 years or multiple life sentences, the point that I am attempting to make here in our discussion is that, just because your body is confined, your mind or your "true-self" does not have to be. What is your "true-self"? Your "true-self" is your spirit, it's your indwelling intelligence. It's that essence that is there with you when you go to sleep, that which awakens you in the morning and is with you throughout your day. It's your unlimited potential to "become".

I may be getting a little philosophical here, but you know what I am saying is true. Never give up! Never diminish your potential. If you have a life sentence then do something to help someone else. Study law, educate yourself. Just because you're "in" doesn't mean you can't help others who are on the outside. If you have that long sentence or if you are even on "death row"—then write a book, write something to convey your thoughts, feelings, and experiences.

Do something to help somebody. Leave a legacy of positivity—don't just sit there—don't give up!

Building A Track Record

Anyone serving time should be building a track record. It should be obvious what a "track record" is, and it should be equally understandable that a "track record" can be of a positive or negative nature.

A negative track record, equals regular disciplinary reports in your file and constantly going in and out of the "hole". No classes or programs completed; so, needless to say, you know what the outcome will be when it's time for you to go before the parole board. Don't get pissed off when you get turned down—"you get what your hand calls for".

A positive track record; equals respect. When I say respect, I mean not only from staff but, from all others around you who are also locked up.

When a person "walks his/her talk", that, in and of itself demands respect. When a person emits a positive and constructive attitude that is what's returned to them.

Anyone can detect a phony or fake, especially in the prison houses. People see you on a day-to-day basis and watch you even though you don't know you're being watched.

A "positive track record" is established when your case-worker opens your file and has paperwork and certificates proving how many educational courses you have completed, how many college degrees you have obtained, how many self-help programs you have completed, how many trades you have been certified in and what your overall attitude and adjustment to prison life has been.

Please hear my true message: In no way am I suggesting that all you need to do is do everything you are supposed to, follow all the rules, and that when you go before the parole board that you are going to "walk". It might happen, but it didn't for me. On the last twenty year sentence that I did, I was scheduled to go before the parole board once every three years. Of course, when I went before the first parole hearing after 3 years of "serving time" and following all the rules and taking some educational classes, I felt pretty good about " getting out". I even had family support behind me.

Yet, when I went up before the parole board, I was told by them that they commended me on doing a good job thus far but because of the type of sentence that I had, and because it was my second twenty year sentence for armed bank robbery the parole board decided to give me another 3 year hit. I faced another 3 long years before I could even think about going back before the parole board.

Yeah, I was crushed and pissed-off, at least on the surface of my thoughts. I thought: "what the hell, what good is doing right going to do"? However, deep down inside, I knew I had to push down the anger and re-channel the hostility.

At that point I decided to "pump it up a notch." I went to work in the cotton mill at the Atlanta Federal Penitentiary. I worked day and night; I worked overtime for seven months straight, which allowed me to save up over a thousand dollars.

Then I waited for the next college semester to start and signed up for every college class I could take. I was secretary of AA, I was involved in just about all the religious groups and various other programs within the institution. I was determined to "out shine" anyone else in the entire institution by way of programming and discipline. This was the approach that met with success in terms of gaining my freedom.

Furloughs

In many prison institutions there are policies that allows an individual who is incarcerated in a maximum-security environment to be down graded to medium security and then even down to minimum security. At minimum security you are allowed to have furloughs. A furlough allows you to be able to go home to family for two or three days, and then return to prison.

Work Release

You also, have what's known as work release. This is a program designed by the prison to allow you to go out of the prison to work for various companies in order to earn money to help and prepare you for your reintegration into the outside society. But, none of this happens without a good "track record".

One Day And A Wake-Up

This is the day before the day when you are actually released. So, you've made parole, or maybe you didn't, maybe you served all of the time that you were sentenced for and don't even have to be on parole; whatever the case, you are about to regain your freedom.

These couple of days can be filled with anxiety because, for one you're so close to being "out" of prison, yet, on the other hand, you wonder if somebody is going to try to keep you there with them by causing you do something which will destroy your chances of getting “out”. My suggestion to you is to continue to stay positively focused and you *will* walk out of those prison doors!

How Have You Prepared Yourself For Freedom?

So, this is the morning that you've been waiting for, for so long. Over the loud speaker you hear your name called to report to R & D with “bag and baggage”. You are going out the same way that you came in. That's why it's called R & D (receiving and discharge).

Now, the question you have to ask yourself is, what have you done to prepare yourself for the “outside world”? How can you be productive in society and stay out of the confines of the prison in the future? I hope you have the answers long before you get to R & D, if not... there's a pretty good chance that you will be back! Do you remember the goal setting that we discussed in an earlier chapter?

Home?
Or The Halfway House?

It may be apparent that going home can be a bit more advantageous to your reintegration back into society. That is if you are going into an environment that promotes growth, caring and support. If you're going home to a "crack house" or a house of "ill repute", with no stability, then you are just fooling yourself. You will be back in the penitentiary in no time flat. Remember, that association brings about assimilation. You just have to be there, and "*not even be indulging*", but, you're in the wrong place at the wrong time, when the "heat" comes down.

Often times it's good to change environments. I got permission before I was "out" on parole to leave Baltimore City, MD. and move to Ohio. I was still on paper; five years of reporting to my parole officer every month. I know, without a doubt, that my new environment allowed me to really start fresh.

The Half Way House

This is a facility designed to sustain the person who is being released from prison. Just as the name implies, halfway house—means you are half way "out". When you agree to go to a half way house there are still rules that have to be followed, such as curfew, seeking employment, attending various programs, etc. If there are infractions to these rules you can be sent back to prison. Obviously, a half way house is better, by far, than being in the penitentiary.

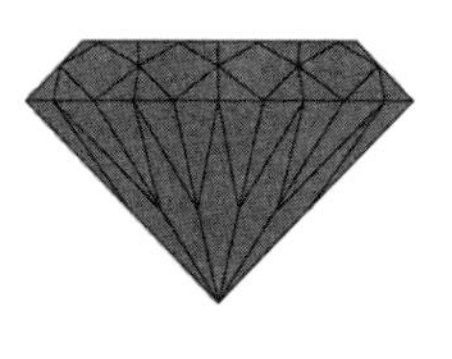

The Metamorphosis The Caterpillar, A Piece Of Coal

The word metamorphosis as defined by Webster's Collegiate Dictionary (tenth addition) 1: transformation and change in the structure and habits of an animal during normal growth.

The Caterpillar

Let's take a look at the caterpillar. This worm-like creature crawls on its belly, close to the ground, subject to be stepped on or trampled on at any given time by the larger and more powerful creatures around it. But, there comes a point in time when the little worm gets tired of crawling around on its belly and begins to transform itself.

The little worm goes to work, building a cocoon and that caterpillar is enclosed in that cocoon (prison) for quite some time. But while in that cocoon, a positive change is being made; a transformation is taking place. At the appointed time the cocoon (prison walls) can no longer hold what's inside, and what bursts forth is a butterfly. A thing of beauty, that flies high above the very ground it once crawled upon. Everyone respects the beauty of the "butterfly".

A Piece Of Coal

That old dusty, black piece of coal. It's good to use for starting fires and burning up. It's very expendable. But, you know, that same old piece of coal (if placed under tremendous pressure for a long period of time i.e.,(prison confinement) becomes a radiant "diamond". In some cases the diamond is deemed priceless or at least admired and desired by all who sees it. Can you grasp my point? You are that caterpillar or that piece of coal. While in prison you must not be satisfied with just "doing your time". By no means, you must undergo a metamorphosis and become that "flying butterfly" or that "radiant diamond". You have all that potential. It's inside of you—go and pull it out. Focus and be disciplined.

In closing, I want to thank you for honoring me with your time and energy by reading and digesting the thoughts contained in this discussion. I leave you with this thought... Trust the Creator with all your heart; what ever name you may choose to use to identify that Higher Power, then trust yourself to do what's right, and above all, *TO THINE OWN SELF BE TRUE*!

Glossary

1.) Appeal - To take a lower courts decision to a higher court for review.

2.) Case - A situation (charge) requiring investigation or action (as by the police).

3.) Commissary - A prison store where food and other items can be purchased, as in a super market.

4.) C.O. - Corrections Officer, one who is involved in the treatment and rehabilitation of offenders through a program involving penal custody.

5.) Contraband - Illegal or prohibited traffic in goods: smuggling.

6.) Count - Allegation or charge

7.) Count Time - Intervals in which individuals who are in prison are counted for security purposes.

8.) Dear John (male)- A letter in which a wife asks for a divorce or a girlfriend breaks off an engagement or friendship.

9.) Furlough - A leave of absence granted from the penal setting authorizing a home visit.

10.) Goon Squad - Slang for a group of correction officers trained in subduing security threats within the prison setting.

11.) Hack - Slang for a prison guard or C.O.

12.) Halfway House - A residence for formerly institutionalized persons.

13.) Hit - Slang for being turned down at a parole hearing, the time between the next parole hearing.

14.) Hole - Slang name for solitary confinement or segregation a way from the general population for various intervals of time to serve as a punishment for the breaking of rules within the prison setting.

15.) Infirmary - A place where the sick are lodged and cared for.

16.) Jacket - A file that is usually kept by the case worker to track the progress of an individual during their prison stay.

17.) Jailhouse Lawyer- A prisoner who is versed in various aspects of law.

18.) Lifer - A person sentenced to imprisonment for life.

19.) Lock Down - The confinement of prisoners to their cells for all or most of the day as a temporary security measure.

20.) Maximum Custody - The strictest and most confining prison setting.

21.) Medium Custody - A middle condition or degree of penal security between maximum and medium security.

22.) Minimum Custody - The lowest or least amount of confinement or security in a penal setting.

23.) Parole - A conditional release of a prisoner serving an indeterminate or unexpired sentence.

24.) Parole Board - A panel of appointed state or federal commissioners who decides whether one will be paroled or not.

25.) Parolee - One who has been granted parole.

26.) Pen Pal - A friend made and kept through letter writing.

27.) Penitentiary - An institution in which offenders of the law are confined, usually state, federally or privately operated.

28.) Probation - The action of suspending the sentence of a convicted offender and giving the offender freedom under the supervision of a probation officer.

29.) Snitch - An informer, usually in concert with prison staff. Frowned upon by other prisoners.

30.) Tank - A large cell, usually consisting of 4 to 8 bunks.

31.) Two-time Loser - One who is sentenced at least twice for the same or different crime.

32.) Warden - An official charged with special supervisory duties or with the enforcement of specified laws or regulations, esp. an official in charge of the operation of a prison.

33.) Work Release - The privilege of allowing one who is incarcerated to leave the prison setting to go to work on the outside for a specified or an allotted time.

ORDER FORM

HOW TO SURVIVE AND EXCEL IN PRISON (WITHIN AND WITHOUT)

ISBN 0-9710607-0-3

$10.59 (price includes 6.5% sales tax)
$11.44 Canadian

Ask for this book at your local bookstore or use this page to order. Please send me this book.

I Am Enclosing $ ______________________________

(Add $3.00 To Cover Postage And Handling).

Send Check Or Money Order, No Cash Or C.O.D.'s, Please.

Name: ______________________________

Address: ______________________________

____

City/State/Zip: ______________________________

Send Order To:

Which Way Is Out? Publications

P.O. Box 26250, Trotwood, Ohio 45426

Allow Four To Six Weeks For Delivery

Prices And Availability Subject To Change Without Notice.